Quest for Knowledge

Seas of Curiosity

By:

Leonard Kenneth,

Olivia Michael

Jane Nicholas

EPISODE ONE

(Ep 1)

In a world where the boundaries of knowledge blur with the vastness of the unknown, Captain Amelia stands as a beacon of curiosity and determination. Her quest begins not in the physical sense, but in the depths of her intellect, where the flames of inquiry burn brightest.

As dawn breaks over the horizon, casting hues of orange and gold upon the restless sea, Captain Amelia stands at the helm of her ship, The Voyager. The salty breeze ruffles her hair as she gazes out towards the distant horizon, her mind already racing ahead to the mysteries that lie beyond.

With each passing day, the crew of The Voyager grows in number and diversity, drawn together by a shared hunger for discovery. Scholars pore over ancient tomes and charts, scientists calibrate their instruments with precision, and adventurers prepare for the trials that lie ahead.

But it is Captain Amelia who stands at the forefront, her determination unyielding in the face of uncertainty. For her, the pursuit of knowledge is not merely a desire, but a calling of a sacred duty to unravel the secrets of the cosmos and illuminate the darkness with the light of understanding.

As The Voyager sets sail into uncharted waters, the crew braces themselves for the challenges that await. From tempestuous storms to treacherous currents, each day brings new obstacles that test their resolve and ingenuity. Yet, with Captain Amelia at the helm, they press on undeterred, their eyes fixed firmly on the horizon.

But as the journey unfolds, it becomes clear that their quest is not without its dangers. Rival adventurers and treasure hunters lurk in the shadows, their motives shrouded in secrecy and deceit. Tensions rise and alliances are tested as Captain Amelia and her crew navigate the treacherous waters of ambition and greed.

Yet, amidst the chaos and uncertainty, moments of clarity emerge epiphanies that illuminate the path forward and reaffirm their purpose. For Captain Amelia and her crew, true wisdom lies not in the accumulation of knowledge, but in the humility to acknowledge the vastness of the unknown.

And so, as The Voyager approaches the fabled Island of Knowledge, Captain Amelia and her crew stand ready to confront whatever mysteries await. For in the end, it is not the destination that defines their journey, but the lessons learned along the way, the epiphanies and reflections that shape their understanding of the world and their place within it.

In the bustling port town of Harbor's End, Captain Amelia begins the daunting task of assembling her crew for the perilous voyage ahead. With a keen eye and discerning judgment, she seeks out individuals whose skills and expertise will complement her own in this quest for knowledge.

First among her recruits is Professor
Marcus, a renowned scholar whose mastery
of ancient languages and civilizations will
prove invaluable in deciphering the
mysteries that lie ahead. His weathered face
bears the marks of a lifetime spent poring
over dusty tomes and crumbling

manuscripts, yet his eyes still burn with the fire of intellectual curiosity.

Next, Captain Amelia seeks out Dr. Isabella, a brilliant scientist whose expertise in navigation and astronomy will guide The Voyager through the treacherous waters of the unknown. With a keen mind and steady hand, she celebrates her instruments with precision, her gaze fixed firmly on the stars above.

As word of Captain Amelia's quest spreads throughout the port, adventurers from far and wide flock to join her crew, eager for the chance to test their mettle against the unknown. Among them is the fearless explorer, Jackson Blake, whose tales of daring escapades and close encounters with mythical creatures have become the stuff of legend.

But it is not just skill and expertise that Captain Amelia seeks in her crew, it is also loyalty and camaraderie, forged through the trials and tribulations of life at sea. And so, as The Voyager prepares to set sail, a diverse and eclectic group of individuals stand ready to embark on this epic journey, a journey that will test their courage, challenge their intellect, and ultimately, redefine their understanding of the world around them.

With the sun hanging low on the horizon, casting a golden hue upon the tranquil waters, Captain Amelia stands at the bow of The Voyager, her gaze fixed on the distant horizon. The moment of departure has finally arrived, and anticipation hums in the air like the taut strings of a finely tuned instrument.

As the crew members bustle about the deck, securing lines and unfurling sails, Captain Amelia's voice rings out clear and commanding above the din. With a nod of her head and a firm grip on the wheel, she gives the signal to cast off, and The Voyager lurches forward, cutting through the gentle waves with grace and determination.

As the coastline recedes into the distance, a sense of exhilaration fills the air, mingling with the salty tang of the sea breeze. The crew stands tall and resolute, their hearts buoyed by the promise of adventure and discovery that lies ahead.

Yet, even as they chart a course into the unknown, Captain Amelia's keen intellect and unwavering resolve serve as a guiding light in the darkness. With each passing mile, she steers The Voyager with precision and purpose, her eyes ever fixed on the distant horizon where the mysteries of the world await.

And so, with the wind at their backs and the stars as their guide, Captain Amelia and her crew set sail into the boundless expanse of the open sea, ready to face whatever challenges and revelations the journey may bring. For in the end, it is not the destination that defines their quest, but the journey itself: the moments of triumph and adversity, the bonds forged in the crucible of adventure, and the unyielding spirit of exploration that propels them ever forward towards the unknown.

As The Voyager cuts through the waves, leaving a foamy wake in its path, the voyage truly begins in earnest. Captain Amelia stands tall at the helm, her steady hands guiding the ship with a practiced ease born of years spent at sea.

The crew members, each finding their place in the rhythm of life onboard, settle into their roles with a sense of purpose and determination. Scholars pore over ancient texts and maps, seeking clues to the island's whereabouts, while scientists conduct experiments and observations, eager to unlock the secrets of the natural world.

Days turn into weeks, and weeks into months, as The Voyager sails ever onward, its bow pointed steadfastly towards the horizon. Along the way, the crew encounters storms and challenges that test their resolve, yet they press on undeterred, fueled by the promise of discovery that lies ahead.

As the days stretch into nights, and the nights into days, bonds are forged among the crew bonds that transcend language and culture, uniting them in a shared sense of purpose and camaraderie. For they know that only by working together can they hope to overcome the obstacles that lie in their path.

And so, as The Voyager continues its journey across the vast expanse of the open sea, the crew remains steadfast in their quest, their hearts filled with hope and determination. For they know that beyond the horizon lies the Island of Knowledge, and with it, the answers to the universe's greatest mysteries.

As The Voyager sails further into uncharted waters, it encounters storms of unparalleled ferocity, each more daunting than the last. Towering waves crash against the ship's hull, threatening to swallow it whole, while howling winds whip through the rigging like vengeful spirits.

Captain Amelia and her crew are tested to their limits as they struggle to navigate through the tempest, their every move dictated by the whims of the merciless sea. Yet, despite the chaos and danger that surrounds them, they stand firm, their resolve unbroken in the face of adversity.

With each passing storm, the crew learns to adapt and improvise, honing their skills and instincts to weather the challenges that lie ahead. They work tirelessly, bailing water, repairing damaged sails, and bracing themselves against the relentless onslaught of nature's fury.

But as the storms rage on, tensions among the crew begin to rise, frayed nerves and weary bodies pushed to the brink of exhaustion. Yet, amidst the chaos and uncertainty, Captain Amelia remains a beacon of strength and leadership, guiding her crew with unwavering determination and courage.

And so, as The Voyager battles through the storms that rage across the open sea, Captain Amelia and her crew stand united against the forces of nature, their spirits unbroken and their resolve unwavering. For they know that beyond the storm lies the calm waters of the Island of Knowledge, and with it, the

promise of discovery and enlightenment.

As The Voyager navigates through the vast expanse of the open sea, the crew's keen eyes and sharp minds uncover a myriad of discoveries that both astonish and intrigue. Amidst the churning waves, they encounter fascinating marine life: pods of playful dolphins dancing in the ship's wake, majestic whales breaching the surface in graceful arcs, and colorful schools of fish darting through the crystal-clear waters below.

But it is not just the creatures of the sea that captivate the crew's attention. They also stumble upon strange phenomena that defy explanation: luminous patches of bioluminescent plankton that shimmer like stars in the night, mysterious whirlpools that seem to defy the laws of physics, and eerie fog banks that cloak the horizon in an ethereal haze.

As the days turn into weeks and the weeks into months, the crew's thirst for discovery only grows stronger. They conduct experiments, collect samples, and record their observations in meticulous detail, eager to unravel the mysteries that surround them.

But amidst the excitement of their discoveries, the crew also faces moments of danger and uncertainty. They must navigate treacherous reefs, navigate treacherous reefs, and avoid the clutches of rival adventurers who seek to claim their findings for themselves.

Yet, through it all, Captain Amelia and her crew remain steadfast in their pursuit of knowledge, their spirits buoyed by the promise of discovery that lies just beyond the horizon. For they know that with each new revelation, they come one step closer to unlocking the secrets of the universe and fulfilling their quest for enlightenment.

As The Voyager sails ever closer to its destination, the atmosphere aboard the ship crackles with anticipation and excitement. The crew stands at the ready, their eyes fixed on the horizon where the faint outline of land begins to emerge from the mist.

Captain Amelia stands at the bow, her heart racing with a mixture of exhilaration and trepidation. For years, the Island of Knowledge has been but a distant dream, a tantalizing promise on the horizon. And now, at long last, it lies within reach.

As The Voyager draws nearer, the crew's senses are overwhelmed by the sights and sounds of the island. Towering cliffs rise from the sea, their rugged faces etched with the passage of time. Lush forests blanket the landscape, their emerald hues beckoning like a siren's song. But it is not just the island's natural beauty that captivates the crew's attention. They also catch glimpses of ancient ruins and mysterious structures nestled among the foliage remnants of a civilization long since vanished.

As The Voyager approaches the shore, Captain Amelia gives the order to drop anchor, and the crew springs into action, preparing to disembark and explore this enigmatic island that holds the promise of untold knowledge and discovery.

Yet, even as they set foot on solid ground, a sense of unease hangs in the air. For they know that the island holds secrets far greater and more profound than they ever imagined, and that their journey is far from over. But with Captain Amelia leading the way, they stand ready to face whatever challenges and revelations await them on the Island of Knowledge.

As the crew of The Voyager sets foot on the Island of Knowledge, they are greeted by a sense of awe and wonder that permeates the very air. Every step they take reveals new mysteries waiting to be unraveled, new secrets waiting to be discovered.

Exploring the ancient ruins that dot the landscape, they uncover clues to the island's enigmatic past carvings and inscriptions that speak of a civilization long forgotten, of knowledge lost to the sands of time.

But it is not just the island's history that captivates their attention. As they delve deeper into its hidden chambers and forgotten tombs, they stumble upon artifacts of incredible power and significant relics that hint at the island's true purpose and the secrets it holds.

Yet, even as they uncover these marvels, the crew is not immune to the island's dangers. They encounter traps and pitfalls designed to

ensnare the unwary, and strange creatures that lurk in the shadows, guardians of the island's mysteries.

But through it all, Captain Amelia and her crew press on, their determination unyielding in the face of adversity. For they know that with each new discovery, they come one step closer to unlocking the secrets of the universe and fulfilling their quest for knowledge.

And so, as they unravel the mysteries of the Island of Knowledge, Captain Amelia and her crew stand on the threshold of enlightenment, ready to confront whatever challenges and revelations await them in the days ahead. For they know that true wisdom

lies not just in the answers they seek, but in

the journey they undertake to find them.

As the crew of The Voyager continues their exploration of the Island of Knowledge, they encounter trials and tribulations that test their resolve and ingenuity to the limit.

Amidst the ancient ruins, they face puzzles and riddles that guard the island's secrets, each more intricate and perplexing than the last. They must decipher cryptic inscriptions, navigate labyrinthine passageways, and unlock hidden chambers to uncover the truth hidden within.

But the challenges they face are not merely physical. As tensions among the crew reach a boiling point, they must also confront their

inner demons and personal conflicts.

Betrayals and mistrust threaten to tear them

apart, forcing Captain Amelia to navigate

treacherous waters both on land and at sea.

Yet, amidst the chaos and uncertainty,

moments of unity and camaraderie emerge.

The crew rallies together, drawing strength from one another in the face of adversity. Bonds forged in the crucible of hardship grow stronger, as they realize that only by working together can they hope to overcome the challenges that lie ahead.

And so, with determination in their hearts and a steadfast resolve, Captain Amelia and her crew press on, undeterred by the trials and tribulations that stand in their way. For they know that true wisdom is not bestowed upon the faint of heart, but earned through perseverance and courage in the face of adversity.

As Captain Amelia and her crew delve deeper into the mysteries of the Island of Knowledge, they realize that their ultimate quest is not merely to uncover its secrets, but to understand the true nature of knowledge itself.

Guided by the island's ancient texts and enigmatic artifacts, they embark on a journey of intellectual and spiritual discovery, seeking answers to questions that have puzzled humanity for millennia.

But the path they tread is fraught with peril, as they confront the limits of human understanding and the ethical dilemmas that arise when the pursuit of knowledge clashes with the pursuit of power.

As they delve deeper into the island's mysteries, they come to realize that true wisdom lies not in the accumulation of knowledge, but in the humility to acknowledge the vastness of the unknown.

And so, with this newfound understanding guiding their every step, Captain Amelia and her crew continue their quest, their hearts filled with a sense of purpose and a determination to seek out the truths that lie beyond the horizon.

For they know that the ultimate quest for knowledge is not a journey with a final destination, but a lifelong pursuit, a journey that will lead them to the farthest reaches of the cosmos and the deepest depths of the human soul.

As The Voyager sets sail once more, leaving the Island of Knowledge behind, Captain Amelia and her crew carry with them the memories of their epic journey and the lessons they have learned along the way.

As they return to civilization, they are greeted as heroes, their tales of adventure and discovery inspiring awe and admiration in all who hear them. Yet, amidst the celebrations and accolades, there is a sense of somber reflection, a realization that their quest for knowledge is far from over.

For Captain Amelia and her crew, the journey has been not just a physical one, but a spiritual and intellectual odyssey: a quest to understand the true nature of the universe and their place within it.

As they disembark from The Voyager and step onto solid ground once more, they do so with a renewed sense of purpose and a determination to continue their pursuit of knowledge, wherever it may lead them.

And so, as they bid farewell to the open sea and the boundless horizon that stretches beyond, Captain Amelia and her crew set forth on a new journey, a journey of discovery, enlightenment, and the endless pursuit of truth. For they know that true wisdom lies not in the destination, but in the journey itself and theirs is a journey that will

never truly end.

EPISODE ONE

Ep 2

In the heart of a bustling port town, where the salty scent of the sea mingles with the cries of seagulls, Captain Amelia stands on the deck of her ship, The Voyager. The morning sun casts a warm glow over the harbor, illuminating the sturdy vessel and its eager crew.

For Captain Amelia, this is not just another journey, it is the culmination of a lifetime of dreams and aspirations. Fuelled by an insatiable thirst for knowledge and a boundless spirit of adventure, she has spent years preparing for this moment.

As she looks out at the horizon, her mind races with the possibilities that lie ahead. The Island of Knowledge beckons like a distant mirage, its secrets shrouded in mystery and intrigue. With each passing moment, the anticipation builds, propelling her ever closer to the journey that awaits.

But Captain Amelia is not alone in her quest. Alongside her stands a fearless crew of scholars, scientists, and adventurers, each driven by their own thirst for discovery. Together, they will embark on a voyage into the unknown, braving storms and challenges in search of the truth that lies beyond.

And so, as The Voyager sets sail, its sails billowing in the wind and its bow pointed towards the horizon, Captain Amelia and her crew embark on a journey that will change their lives forever. For theirs is not just a voyage across the sea, it is a quest for knowledge, a quest for enlightenment, and a quest for the very essence of what it means to be human.

In the heart of Harbor's End, where the sea breeze carries tales of distant lands and untold adventures, Captain Amelia begins the arduous task of assembling her crew for the epic voyage ahead.

First to join her ranks is Professor Marcus, a venerable scholar whose expertise in ancient languages and civilizations is unmatched. With his weathered face and piercing gaze, he brings a wealth of knowledge that will prove invaluable on their quest.

Next, Captain Amelia seeks out Dr. Isabella, a brilliant navigator and astronomer whose keen intellect and steady hand will guide

The Voyager through the treacherous waters they are destined to face. With her charts and sextants in hand, she eagerly accepts the call to adventure.

As word of Captain Amelia's quest spreads throughout the port, adventurers from all walks of life flock to join her crew, drawn by the promise of discovery and the thrill of the unknown. Among them is Jackson Blake, a fearless explorer whose tales of daring escapades have become the stuff of legend.

But Captain Amelia knows that a successful voyage requires more than just skill and expertise; it requires trust, loyalty, and a shared sense of purpose. And so, as The Voyager prepares to set sail, a diverse and eclectic group of individuals stand ready to embark on this epic journey, a journey that will test their courage, challenge their intellect, and ultimately, redefine their understanding of the world around them.

With the crew assembled and The Voyager prepared for the journey ahead, Captain Amelia and her companions face the daunting task of charting uncharted waters. Guided by ancient maps and whispered legends, they set their course into the unknown, eager to explore the mysteries that lie beyond the horizon.

As they sail deeper into uncharted territory, the crew encounters challenges that test their courage and resourcefulness. Treacherous reefs lurk beneath the surface, hidden shoals threaten to ground the ship, and unpredictable currents pull them off course.

Yet, with Captain Amelia's steady hand at the helm and the crew's unwavering determination, they press on undeterred. They navigate through narrow channels and treacherous passages, their eyes fixed on the distant horizon where the promise of discovery awaits.

As they chart their course, they also encounter wonders beyond their wildest imagination. They witness breathtaking sunsets that paint the sky in hues of orange and gold, encounter exotic creatures that frolic in the waves, and marvel at the beauty of remote islands that dot the seascape.

But amidst the beauty and wonder, danger lurks around every corner. Storms rage with fury, threatening to tear The Voyager apart, and unknown perils lurk beneath the surface, waiting to ensnare the unwary.

Yet, despite the challenges they face, Captain Amelia and her crew remain undaunted in their quest. For they know that beyond the uncharted waters lies the promise of discovery, adventure, and the fulfillment of their wildest dreams. And with each passing day, they draw closer to the ultimate destination, the Island of Knowledge, where the answers to their questions await.

As The Voyager ventures deeper into uncharted waters, it encounters fierce storms that test the crew's mettle like never before. Dark clouds loom on the horizon, swirling ominously as the wind picks up and waves rise to monstrous heights.

Captain Amelia stands at the helm, her grip firm on the wheel as she steers the ship through the tempest. Rain lashes against the deck, and lightning splits the sky, illuminating the chaos that surrounds them.

The crew scrambles to secure the sails and batten down the hatches, their faces etched with determination as they face the fury of the elements. With each crash of thunder and roll of thunder, their resolve is tested, yet they stand firm, united in their determination to weather the storm.

But as the tempest rages on, the crew's resources are stretched to their limits. The ship groans and creaks under the strain, and fatigue sets in as the relentless onslaught shows no sign of abating.

Yet, amidst the chaos and danger, a sense of camaraderie emerges among the crew. They draw strength from one another, working together to keep The Voyager afloat and their spirits high.

And finally, after what seems like an eternity, the storm begins to relent. The clouds part, and the sun breaks through, casting a warm glow over the battered ship and its weary crew.

As The Voyager emerges from the storm, battered but unbroken, Captain Amelia and her companions breathe a sigh of relief. They have faced the fiercest of storms and emerged victorious, their spirits undimmed and their resolve stronger than ever. And with each challenge they overcome, they draw one step closer to their ultimate goal, the Island of Knowledge, where the answers to their questions await.

As The Voyager sails deeper into uncharted waters, the crew confronts towering waves that rise like monstrous giants from the depths below. Each swell threatens to engulf the ship, sending it tumbling into the churning sea.

Captain Amelia stands resolute at the helm, her gaze fixed on the horizon as she steers The Voyager through the tumultuous waters. With each wave that crashes against the ship's hull, she braces herself against the wheel, guiding the vessel with unwavering determination.

The crew works tirelessly to keep The Voyager afloat, their muscles straining against the relentless pull of the ocean. They secure the rigging, lash down loose cargo, and bail water from the deck as the ship pitches and rolls beneath their feet.

Yet, despite their efforts, the towering waves seem insurmountable, rising higher and higher with each passing moment. Fear grips the crew's hearts as they struggle to maintain their footing amidst the chaos.

But Captain Amelia refuses to yield to despair. With steely resolve, she rallies her crew, urging them to stand firm in the face of adversity. Together, they weather the storm, drawing strength from one another as they navigate through the towering waves.

And finally, after what feels like an eternity, the sea begins to calm. The waves subside, and a sense of relief washes over the exhausted crew. Though battered and weary, they emerge from the ordeal stronger than ever, their spirits undaunted by the challenges they have faced.

As The Voyager sails on, its bow cutting through the calm waters like a knife, Captain Amelia and her crew know that they have conquered one of the greatest challenges the sea has to offer. And with each wave they overcome, they draw one step closer to their ultimate destination the Island of Knowledge, where the answers to their questions await.

As The Voyager ventures further into uncharted waters, the crew encounters strange phenomena that defy explanation, leaving them in awe and wonder.

One night, the sea is illuminated by a mesmerizing display of bioluminescent plankton, casting an ethereal glow that dances across the waves like a celestial ballet. The crew gathers on deck, spellbound by the beauty of the natural spectacle unfolding before them.

In another instance, they stumble upon a mysterious whirlpool that seems to defy the laws of physics, swirling with an otherworldly energy that sends shivers down their spines. They watch in awe as objects are drawn into its depths, disappearing without a trace.

And then there are the eerie fog banks that blanket the horizon, shrouding The Voyager in a cloak of mist that distorts reality and plays tricks on the mind. Strange shapes loom in the darkness, fleeting glimpses of creatures that seem to exist only in the depths of the imagination.

Yet, amidst the strangeness and uncertainty, Captain Amelia and her crew remain steadfast in their quest for knowledge. They document their observations, collect samples, and analyze data in an attempt to unravel the mysteries that surround them.

For they know that the sea is a vast and wondrous place, filled with secrets waiting to be discovered. And as The Voyager sails on, they are filled with a sense of excitement and anticipation, eager to uncover the truth that lies hidden beneath the surface of the waves.

As The Voyager sails further into uncharted waters, navigating the unknown becomes both a challenge and an adventure for Captain Amelia and her crew.

With no maps to guide them and no charts to follow, they rely on their instincts and ingenuity to chart a course through the unexplored expanse of the sea. Each decision they make is a calculated risk, as they weigh the dangers of unknown reefs and treacherous currents against the promise of new discoveries.

But amidst the uncertainty, there is also a sense of excitement and anticipation. Every new day brings the possibility of encountering something never before seen by human eyes: a new species of marine life, a hidden island, or a forgotten civilization lost to time.

As they navigate through fog-shrouded channels and narrow passages, Captain Amelia and her crew rely on their trust in one another and their unwavering determination to press forward. They work together as a well-oiled machine, each member of the crew playing their part in the journey into the unknown.

And as The Voyager sails on, leaving a wake of foamy white in its path, Captain

Amelia and her crew embrace the thrill of exploration and the exhilaration of discovery. For in the vast expanse of the open sea, the possibilities are endless, and the journey itself is the greatest adventure of all.

As The Voyager continues its journey through uncharted waters, Captain Amelia and her crew face trials that test their resolve and ingenuity to the utmost.

One such trial comes when they encounter a series of treacherous reefs that block their path forward. With no clear route to navigate through, the crew must rely on their wits and resourcefulness to find a way around the obstacles. They work tirelessly, using ropes and pulleys to maneuver The Voyager through narrow channels and shallow waters, inching their way forward with painstaking precision.

Another trial presents itself when The Voyager becomes becalmed in the doldrums, the wind disappearing entirely and leaving the ship stranded in the middle of the sea. With supplies dwindling and morale sinking, Captain Amelia must rally her crew and devise a plan to escape the grip of the stagnant air. Through sheer determination and ingenuity, they fashion makeshift sails from spare canvas and rigging, harnessing the slightest breeze to propel The Voyager forward once more.

But perhaps the greatest trial of all comes when the crew's unity is tested by internal discord and strife. Tensions flare as personalities clash and tempers fray, threatening to tear the fragile fabric of camaraderie apart. Yet, through patience and understanding, Captain Amelia fosters a spirit of cooperation and teamwork among her crew, turning conflict into opportunity and discord into harmony.

And so, as The Voyager presses on through the trials and tribulations of the journey, Captain Amelia and her crew emerge stronger and more resilient than ever before. For they know that true strength lies not in avoiding adversity, but in confronting it head-on with courage, determination, and unwavering resolve.

As The Voyager sails through uncharted
waters, adversity becomes an unwelcome
companion, testing the crew's perseverance
and resilience at every turn.

When supplies run low and rations grow
sparse, Captain Amelia and her crew refuse
to succumb to despair. They ration their
provisions wisely, stretching every last scrap
of food and drop of water to its limits. With
ingenuity and resourcefulness, they turn to
fishing and foraging to supplement their
dwindling supplies, determined to weather
the storm of scarcity.

In the face of fierce storms and towering waves, The Voyager becomes a battleground between man and nature. Yet, Captain Amelia and her crew refuse to yield to the fury of the elements. They stand united against the tempest, bracing themselves against the wind and rain, and working tirelessly to keep the ship afloat amidst the chaos.

And when morale threatens to falter in the wake of setbacks and challenges, Captain Amelia becomes a beacon of hope and inspiration for her crew. With her unwavering optimism and indomitable spirit, she rallies her companions, reminding them of the purpose that drives them forward the quest for knowledge and enlightenment.

Through perseverance and determination, Captain Amelia and her crew navigate through the darkest of times, emerging from each trial stronger and more resilient than before. For they know that true greatness is not measured by the absence of adversity, but by the ability to persevere in the face of it. And as The Voyager sails ever onward, they do so with hearts full of courage and minds set on the horizon, ready to confront whatever challenges lie ahead.

As they sails on, the quest for understanding becomes the guiding light for Captain Amelia and her crew. They are driven not just by the desire for knowledge, but by a deeper yearning to unravel the mysteries of the universe and to comprehend their place within it.

With each new discovery and revelation, they delve deeper into the realms of science, history, and philosophy, seeking to unlock the secrets that lie hidden beneath the surface of the world. They pore over ancient texts and artifacts, deciphering cryptic inscriptions and piecing together fragments of lost civilizations in their quest for enlightenment.

But the quest for understanding is not just an intellectual pursuit, it is also a spiritual journey, a search for meaning and purpose in a vast and mysterious cosmos. Captain Amelia and her crew grapple with existential questions and philosophical dilemmas, wrestling with the fundamental mysteries of existence and the nature of reality itself.

And as they sail ever closer to their ultimate destination, the fabled Island of Knowledge they come to realize that true understanding lies not just in the accumulation of facts and figures, but in the wisdom to recognize the limits of human knowledge and the humility to embrace the unknown.

For Captain Amelia and her crew, the quest for understanding is not just a journey it is a way of life, a never ending pursuit of truth and enlightenment that transcends time and space. And as they sail into the unknown, their hearts filled with curiosity and wonder, they know that the greatest discoveries are yet to come.

As they set sail once more, leaving the Island of Knowledge behind, Captain Amelia and her crew find themselves reflecting on the journey that has brought them to this moment.

They have faced trials and tribulations, storms and challenges, yet through it all, they have emerged stronger and more united than ever before. They have delved into the depths of the unknown, seeking answers to the universe's greatest mysteries, and in the process, they have discovered truths that transcend the boundaries of time and space.

But as they look back on their journey, they realize that the true treasure they have found lies not in the artifacts they have unearthed or the knowledge they have gained, but in the bonds of friendship and camaraderie that have been forged along the way.

For in the end, it is not the destination that defines their quest, but the journey itself: the moments of triumph and adversity, the laughter and tears shared among friends, and the profound sense of wonder that has filled their hearts with each new discovery.

And so, as The Voyager sails on towards the horizon, Captain Amelia and her crew carry with them the memories of their epic journey, knowing that the greatest adventure of all is the journey of self-discovery, the quest for understanding, and the boundless exploration of the human spirit.

EPISODE THREE

Ep 3

As the sun rises over the horizon, casting a golden glow upon the tranquil waters, Captain Amelia stands on the deck of The Voyager, her gaze fixed on the distant horizon. The time has come for a new chapter in their epic journey.

With the wind at their backs and the stars as their guide, Captain Amelia and her crew set sail once more into the boundless expanse of the open sea. They carry with them the memories of their past adventures, the lessons they have learned, and the bonds that have been forged through trials and triumphs.

But this is not the end of their story, it is only the beginning. For as The Voyager cuts through the waves, leaving a foamy wake in its path, Captain Amelia and her crew embark on a new quest, filled with excitement, uncertainty, and the promise of new discoveries that await them on the horizon.

And so, with hearts full of hope and spirits ablaze with determination, they sail ever onwards, ready to face whatever challenges and revelations the journey may bring. For theirs is a journey of exploration, enlightenment, and the eternal quest for knowledge that will continue to guide them through the uncharted waters of the

unknown.

As they continue their journey across the vast expanse of the sea, Captain Amelia and her crew encounter mythical creatures said to inhabit the depths of the ocean. Each encounter both captivates and terrifies, fueling the crew's sense of wonder and driving them ever forward in their quest for knowledge.

One moonlit night, they spot the graceful silhouette of a mermaid, her shimmering tail gliding through the water with effortless grace. The crew watches in awe as she sings a haunting melody, her voice echoing across the waves, before disappearing into the depths once more.

Another day, they catch sight of a majestic sea serpent, its scales glistening in the sunlight as it coils and twists through the water. Despite its fearsome appearance, the creature shows no aggression towards The Voyager, passing by with a sense of ancient wisdom and mystery.

And then there are the elusive sirens, whose enchanting songs lure sailors to their doom with promises of eternal bliss. The crew hears their haunting melodies carried on the wind, but Captain Amelia's steely resolve and quick thinking prevent them from falling prey to their seductive charms.

With each mythical encounter, the crew's fascination with the wonders of the ocean deepens, driving them ever onward in their quest. For they know that beyond the realm of human understanding lies a world filled with ancient secrets and untold mysteries,

waiting to be uncovered by those brave

enough to seek them out.

As they sails through the vast expanse of the sea, Captain Amelia and her crew encounter majestic sea serpents, creatures of legend said to inhabit the deepest reaches of the ocean.

One day, as the crew scans the horizon for signs of land, they spot a massive silhouette gliding through the water, a sea serpent of breathtaking size and beauty. Its scales shimmer in the sunlight, casting rainbow hues across the waves as it moves with a grace that belies its massive bulk.

The crew watches in awe as the sea serpent passes by The Voyager, its presence filling them with a sense of wonder and reverence.

Despite its fearsome appearance, the creature shows no hostility towards the ship, content to go about its mysterious business in the depths below.

As the sea serpent disappears beneath the waves, the crew is left speechless, their hearts filled with a mixture of excitement and trepidation. For they have witnessed firsthand the majesty of these legendary creatures, and they know that their encounter marks a momentous milestone in their journey of discovery.

And so, with a newfound sense of awe and respect for the wonders of the ocean,

Captain Amelia and her crew continue their voyage, ever vigilant for the next mythical encounter that awaits them on the horizon.

As they sails through the azure waters, Captain Amelia and her crew catch glimpses of elusive merfolk, beings of myth and legend said to dwell beneath the waves.

One morning, as the crew goes about their duties, they hear strange melodies echoing across the water. Intrigued, they peer over the railings to see a group of merfolk swimming alongside The Voyager, their shimmering tails glinting in the sunlight.

The merfolk watch the ship with curious eyes, their expressions a mix of fascination and caution. They move with a fluid grace, darting in and out of the waves with effortless agility, before disappearing beneath the surface once more.

Despite their fleeting appearance, the crew is captivated by the beauty and mystery of the merfolk. Some believe them to be benevolent spirits, while others warn of their trickster nature, capable of luring sailors to their doom with their enchanting songs.

But Captain Amelia remains steadfast in her resolve, treating the merfolk with respect and caution. She knows that their encounter is a rare and precious opportunity to glimpse a world beyond the realm of human understanding, a world of magic and wonder that exists just beneath the surface of the sea.

And so, as The Voyager continues its journey, the crew carries with them the memory of their encounter with the elusive merfolk, a reminder of the mysteries that lie hidden beneath the waves, waiting to be discovered by those brave enough to seek them out.

As they sails on, Captain Amelia and her crew share tales of ancient legends passed down through generations, stories that speak of forgotten civilizations, mythical creatures, and lost treasures waiting to be discovered.

One such tale tells of a legendary city hidden beneath the waves, its towers and palaces carved from coral and adorned with pearls of unimaginable beauty. According to the legend, the city is guarded by merfolk and sea serpents, its secrets known only to those brave enough to venture into its depths.

Another tale speaks of a powerful artifact known as the Heart of the Ocean, said to possess the ability to control the tides and summon storms at will. It is said to lie hidden on a remote island, guarded by ancient guardians and protected by powerful enchantments.

And then there are the stories of heroic adventurers who braved the perils of the sea in search of fame and fortune. From legendary pirates who plundered the high seas to intrepid explorers who charted unknown territories, their exploits have become the stuff of legend, inspiring awe and admiration in all who hear their tales.

As The Voyager sails on, Captain Amelia and her crew listen to these stories with rapt attention, their imaginations ignited by the promise of adventure and discovery that lies just beyond the horizon. For they know that in the vast expanse of the open sea, the line between myth and reality is often blurred, and that sometimes, the greatest treasures are found in the stories we tell.

As they sails through uncharted waters, Captain Amelia and her crew experience moments of both captivation and terror, each encounter with the unknown stirring a complex mix of emotions within them.

There are moments of captivation, when the crew is spellbound by the beauty and wonder of the natural world. They marvel at the breathtaking sunsets that paint the sky in hues of orange and gold, and the bioluminescent creatures that illuminate the darkness with their ethereal glow. These moments fill them with a sense of awe and reverence for the mysteries of the ocean.

But amidst the beauty, there are also moments of terror, when the crew comes face to face with the dangers that lurk beneath the waves. They encounter fierce storms that threaten to tear The Voyager apart, and strange creatures that haunt their dreams with their otherworldly presence. These moments fill them with fear and trepidation, reminding them of the fragility of their existence in the vast and unpredictable expanse of the open sea.

Yet, amidst the captivation and terror, Captain Amelia and her crew find strength in their unity and determination. They stand together in the face of adversity, drawing courage from one another as they navigate through the trials and tribulations of their journey. And with each passing day, they grow ever closer to their ultimate destination the Island of Knowledge, where the answers to their questions await, and where the line between cavitation and terror blurs into the boundless expanse of the unknown.

As The Voyager sails onward, the quest

for knowledge becomes the driving force

behind Captain Amelia and her crew's

journey. Every discovery, every encounter,

fuels their insatiable thirst to uncover the

secrets of the universe.

They pore over ancient manuscripts,

deciphering cryptic texts in search of clues

that will lead them closer to the truth. They

study the stars, charting their course by the

light of distant galaxies in their quest to

unlock the mysteries of the cosmos.

Each encounter with mythical creatures or

legendary landmarks serves to deepen their

understanding of the world around them, fueling their curiosity and inspiring new avenues of exploration.

But it is not just the pursuit of knowledge that drives them forward, it is the belief that with knowledge comes power, and with power comes the ability to shape the course of their own destiny.

And so, as The Voyager sails ever onward, Captain Amelia and her crew remain steadfast in their determination to seek out the answers that lie beyond the horizon. For they know that true wisdom is not found in the destination, but in the journey itself a journey fueled by the boundless curiosity and unquenchable thirst for knowledge that burns within their hearts.

As The Voyager sails through the realm where myth and reality intertwine, Captain Amelia and her crew find themselves reflecting on the blurred lines between the two.

They ponder the ancient legends they have encountered, wondering how much truth lies hidden within the tales passed down through generations. They marvel at the mythical creatures they have glimpsed, questioning whether they are merely figments of imagination or manifestations of something greater.

But amidst the wonder of myth, they also confront the harsh realities of the world around them. They witness the destructive power of storms and the unforgiving nature of the sea, reminding them of the fragility of human existence in the face of nature's wrath.

Yet, even as they grapple with the complexities of myth and reality, Captain Amelia and her crew find solace in the knowledge that the two are not mutually exclusive. They embrace the mysteries of the unknown, knowing that sometimes, the greatest truths are found in the spaces between fact and fiction.

And so, as The Voyager sails ever onward, they continue to navigate the waters where myth and reality converge, guided by their unwavering curiosity and their steadfast belief in the power of knowledge to illuminate the darkest corners of the human experience.

With reflections on myth and reality lingering in their minds, Captain Amelia and her crew press on with unwavering determination, continuing their voyage across the boundless expanse of the sea.

They set their course towards the distant horizon, propelled by a shared sense of purpose and a thirst for discovery that knows no bounds. Each day brings new challenges and new wonders, as they navigate through storms and calm seas alike, their eyes fixed on the ever-changing landscape before them.

As they sail onward, Captain Amelia and her crew draw strength from the bonds of friendship and camaraderie that have been forged through their shared experiences. They support one another through moments of doubt and uncertainty, celebrating each triumph and facing each setback with resilience and determination.

And though the journey ahead is fraught with unknown dangers and mysteries waiting to be unraveled, they sail on undeterred, fueled by the knowledge that their quest for knowledge is a journey without end a journey that will lead them to the farthest reaches of the cosmos and the deepest depths of the human soul.

For Captain Amelia and her crew, the voyage is not just a means to an end, it is a way of life, a never-ending pursuit of truth and enlightenment that will continue to guide them through the uncharted waters of the unknown, wherever they may lead.

As The Voyager sails on, Captain Amelia and her crew remain steadfast in their pursuit of truth and understanding, driven by an unquenchable thirst for knowledge that knows no bounds.

They delve into ancient texts and decipher cryptic inscriptions, piecing together fragments of lost civilizations in their quest to uncover the mysteries of the past. They study the stars and the natural world, seeking to unlock the secrets of the universe and their place within it.

But their pursuit is not just an intellectual one, it is also a journey of the heart and soul, a search for meaning and purpose in a world filled with uncertainty and chaos. They grapple with existential questions and philosophical dilemmas, wrestling with the fundamental mysteries of existence and the nature of reality itself.

And yet, amidst the complexity and uncertainty, they find solace in the pursuit itself. For they know that true understanding lies not just in the accumulation of facts and figures, but in the wisdom to recognize the limits of human knowledge and the humility to embrace the unknown.

As The Voyager sails ever onward, Captain Amelia and her crew remain guided by their unyielding commitment to truth and understanding, knowing that their journey is not just a destination, but a way of life a never-ending quest for enlightenment that will continue to shape their lives and their destinies for generations to come.

They learn the importance of resilience in the face of adversity, as they weather storms and face challenges that test their mettle. They discover the power of teamwork and cooperation, as they come together to overcome obstacles that would be insurmountable alone.

They learn humility in the face of the unknown, as they confront the limits of human knowledge and the vastness of the mysteries that lie beyond. They gain a deeper appreciation for the interconnectedness of all life, as they witness the delicate balance of the natural world and their place within it.

But perhaps most importantly, they learn the value of friendship and camaraderie, as they forge bonds that withstand the trials and tribulations of their journey. They find strength in each other, drawing courage from the unwavering support and companionship that sustains them through the darkest of times.

And as The Voyager sails on, Captain Amelia and her crew carry these lessons with them, knowing that they will serve as guiding lights in the ever-changing seas of life. For in the end, it is not just the destination that matters, but the journey itself and the lessons learned along the way that shape who we are and who we will become.

EPISODE FOUR

Ep 4

As The Voyager sets sail once more, a new challenge looms on the horizon for Captain Amelia and her intrepid crew. Rival adventurers and treasure hunters, driven by greed and ambition, seek to claim the Island of Knowledge for themselves, threatening to thwart their quest at every turn.

With tensions rising and betrayals lurking in the shadows, Captain Amelia must navigate a treacherous sea of rivalries and conflicts, outwitting and outmaneuvering her foes as they vie for control of the fabled island.

But as the stakes grow higher and the danger mounts, Captain Amelia and her crew must also confront the moral dilemmas that arise when the pursuit of knowledge clashes with the pursuit of power.

For in the end, the true challenge they face is not just the rival adventurers who seek to thwart their quest, but the inner demons that threaten to consume them if they lose sight of the values that define who they are and what they stand for.

And so, as The Voyager sails ever onward, Captain Amelia and her crew brace themselves for the challenges that lie ahead, knowing that the true test of their mettle will not be in the battles they fight or the treasures they seek, but in the choices they make and the principles they uphold along

the way.

As they continue their journey, the identities of the rival adventurers are revealed, adding a new layer of complexity to Captain Amelia's quest for knowledge.

Among them is the notorious Captain Blackbeard, a fearsome pirate known for his ruthless tactics and insatiable greed. With a crew of cutthroats and mercenaries at his command, he will stop at nothing to claim the Island of Knowledge and its secrets for himself.

But Captain Amelia also faces competition from the enigmatic Professor von Braun, a brilliant scientist with a thirst for discovery that rivals her own. Armed with advanced technology and a team of loyal followers, he seeks to unlock the mysteries of the island and harness its power for his own nefarious purposes.

And then there is the mysterious Lady Seraphina, a cunning sorceress whose powers of magic and deception pose a formidable threat to Captain Amelia and her crew. With dark forces at her command, she seeks to manipulate events to her advantage, using trickery and illusion to sow discord among her rivals.

As The Voyager sails on, Captain Amelia and her crew find themselves locked in a deadly game of cat and mouse with their rivals, each encounter bringing them one step closer to the ultimate showdown for control of the Island of Knowledge.

But amidst the chaos and conflict, Captain Amelia remains steadfast in her determination to stay true to her principles and uphold the values that define her as a leader. For she knows that the true test of their worth lies not in the treasures they seek, but in the choices they make and the legacy they leave behind.

As The Voyager faces the challenge of rival adventurers, Captain Amelia and her crew must employ all their wit and cunning to outmaneuver their foes and stay ahead in the race for the Island of Knowledge.

With Captain Blackbeard's ruthless piracy threatening their every move, Captain Amelia utilizes her strategic prowess to outwit him at every turn. She navigates treacherous waters, utilizing her knowledge of the sea to evade Blackbeard's traps and ambushes, all while staying one step ahead of his cunning schemes.

Against Professor von Braun's scientific prowess, Captain Amelia relies on her resourcefulness and adaptability. She leverages the unique skills of her crew members, employing their expertise in engineering, navigation, and exploration to overcome the technological advantages of her rival.

And when faced with the magical machinations of Lady Seraphina, Captain Amelia relies on her unwavering resolve and moral clarity to resist the temptations of dark sorcery. She recognizes the illusions and deceptions for what they are, staying true to her principles even in the face of supernatural manipulation.

But perhaps the greatest challenge of all lies in navigating the moral dilemmas that arise when the pursuit of knowledge clashes with the pursuit of power. Captain Amelia must confront her own inner demons and wrestle with the temptation to compromise her values for the sake of victory.

Through it all, Captain Amelia and her crew remain steadfast in their commitment to each other and to the noble ideals that guide their quest. They know that true victory lies not just in reaching the Island of Knowledge, but in doing so with integrity and honor, no matter the challenges they

face along the way.

As The Voyager sails on, tensions among the crew rise as they confront the relentless pursuit of rival adventurers and the mounting pressures of their quest for the Island of Knowledge. In the midst of this turmoil, betrayals unfold, threatening to unravel the fragile bonds that hold Captain Amelia and her crew together.

Whispers of discontent spread through the ranks as doubts and suspicions fester among the crew. Some question Captain Amelia's leadership, while others succumb to the allure of power and riches promised by their rivals. Loyalties are tested, and allegiances are betrayed as hidden agendas come to light.

Amidst this atmosphere of uncertainty and mistrust, Captain Amelia must navigate the treacherous waters of intrigue and deception, unsure who among her crew she can truly trust. She must remain vigilant, constantly on guard against the machinations of their rivals and the dangers posed by traitors in their midst.

But even as tensions rise and betrayals unfold, Captain Amelia refuses to lose sight of her ultimate goal. She remains resolute in her determination to reach the Island of Knowledge, knowing that the answers they seek lie within its ancient ruins and hidden chambers.

And so, as The Voyager sails on through the stormy seas of uncertainty, Captain Amelia and her loyal companions brace themselves for the challenges that lie ahead, knowing that their survival and the success of their quest depends on their ability to weather the storms of betrayal and emerge stronger on the other side.

As The Voyager navigates through turbulent waters and faces the challenges posed by rival adventurers, Captain Amelia and her crew find themselves confronting moral dilemmas that test their principles to the core.

One such dilemma arises when they discover an ancient artifact that could grant unimaginable power to whoever possesses it. Tempted by the allure of its potential, some members of the crew advocate for seizing the artifact for themselves, believing that they alone are worthy of wielding its power. Others, however, caution against such hubris, warning of the dangers of greed

and ambition.

Another moral quandary presents itself

when they encounter a group of indigenous

people living on a remote island. Some

members of the crew argue for exploiting

the island's resources for their own gain,

while others advocate for respecting the sovereignty and autonomy of the indigenous people, recognizing their right to self-determination.

But perhaps the greatest moral dilemma of all comes when Captain Amelia is faced with a choice between sacrificing the safety of her crew to achieve their ultimate goal or abandoning their quest in order to ensure their survival. It is a decision that weighs heavily on her conscience, forcing her to confront the consequences of her actions and the true cost of their journey.

In the end, Captain Amelia and her crew must navigate these moral dilemmas with wisdom and compassion, striving to uphold their values even in the face of temptation and adversity. For they know that true greatness is not measured by the treasures they amass or the victories they achieve, but by the integrity and honor with which they conduct themselves along the way.

As The Voyager draws closer to the Island of Knowledge, the clash between the pursuit of knowledge and the thirst for power reaches its pinnacle, testing Captain Amelia and her crew in ways they never imagined.

On one hand, there are those who see knowledge as a means to enlightenment and understanding, a force for good in the world. Captain Amelia and her loyal companions are driven by a deep-seated desire to uncover the mysteries of the universe, believing that with knowledge comes wisdom and the potential to better humanity.

On the other hand, there are those who seek knowledge as a tool for domination and control, viewing it as a means to achieve their own selfish ambitions. Rival adventurers and treasure hunters, driven by greed and ambition, will stop at nothing to claim the Island of Knowledge and its secrets for themselves, regardless of the consequences.

As The Voyager approaches the island, tensions between these opposing forces reach a boiling point, threatening to erupt into open conflict. Captain Amelia must navigate a delicate balance between her quest for knowledge and the dangers posed by those who would seek to exploit it for their own gain.

In the end, Captain Amelia and her crew must confront the ultimate question: What is the true purpose of their journey? Is it to amass power and wealth at the expense of others, or is it to seek understanding and enlightenment for the betterment of all humanity?

As they stand on the precipice of discovery, Captain Amelia and her crew must choose their path wisely, knowing that the fate of not just their own destinies, but the fate of the entire world, hangs in the balance.

As The Voyager faces the escalating conflict between the pursuit of knowledge and the thirst for power, Captain Amelia and her crew must develop strategies for survival to navigate the treacherous waters ahead.

Captain Amelia emphasizes the importance of unity among the crew, fostering a sense of camaraderie and mutual support. By standing together as a cohesive unit, they are better equipped to withstand external pressures and internal discord.

With rival adventurers and treacherous waters posing constant threats, Captain Amelia ensures that her crew remains vigilant and prepared for any eventuality. They maintain a state of heightened awareness, ready to respond swiftly and decisively to any challenges that arise.

In the face of conflicts with rival adventurers and indigenous peoples, Captain Amelia advocates for diplomacy and negotiation whenever possible. By seeking peaceful resolutions to disputes and conflicts, they can minimize the risk of violence and foster positive relationships with others.

As circumstances change and new challenges emerge, Captain Amelia encourages her crew to remain adaptable and flexible in their approach. They must be willing to adjust their strategies and tactics on the fly, responding creatively to unexpected obstacles and opportunities.

Above all, Captain Amelia emphasizes the importance of ethical decision-making in their quest for knowledge. They must remain true to their principles and values, even in the face of temptation and adversity, choosing the path of integrity and honor no matter the cost.

By employing these strategies for survival, Captain Amelia and her crew stand ready to confront the challenges ahead with courage, determination, and unwavering resolve.

As The Voyager sails through the tumultuous waters of conflict, Captain Amelia and her crew must navigate a complex landscape of allies and enemies, where alliances can shift like the tides and loyalties are constantly put to the test.

Allies: Captain Amelia's steadfast companions, bound by a shared sense of purpose and camaraderie, stand by her side through thick and thin. Together, they form the backbone of The Voyager, supporting each other through the trials and tribulations of their journey. Along their journey, Captain Amelia and her crew may encounter indigenous peoples who inhabit the islands they explore. By forging positive relationships with these communities, they can gain valuable allies who may offer assistance, guidance, and protection. In the midst of conflict, there may be neutral parties who choose not to take sides. Captain Amelia and her crew can leverage their relationships with these individuals or groups to gather information, broker alliances, or negotiate peaceful resolutions to disputes.

Enemies: Chief among The Voyager's enemies are the rival adventurers and treasure hunters who seek to claim the

Island of Knowledge for themselves. Driven by greed and ambition, these adversaries will stop at nothing to thwart Captain Amelia's quest and seize the island's secrets for their own gain. Beyond the machinations of rival adventurers, The Voyager must also contend with the dangers posed by the untamed wilderness and the unpredictable forces of nature. From fierce storms and treacherous reefs to deadly sea creatures, these natural threats can pose significant challenges to the crew's survival. Within their own ranks, Captain Amelia and her crew must remain vigilant against the threat of betrayal and deception. In the high-stakes world of adventure and exploration, loyalties can be tested, and hidden agendas may lurk beneath the surface, posing dangers that are often more insidious than those posed by external enemies.

As Captain Amelia and her crew navigate the complex web of alliances and enmities that define their journey, they must remain steadfast in their principles and resolute in their determination to overcome whatever obstacles stand in their way. For in the end, it is not just the strength of their allies or the cunning of their enemies that will determine their fate, but the courage and resilience of their own hearts.

As The Voyager progresses on its journey, Captain Amelia and her crew uncover hidden agendas that complicate their quest for knowledge and challenge their trust in allies.

Through careful observation and investigation, Captain Amelia and her crew unveil the true intentions of their rival adventurers. They discover that Captain Blackbeard seeks to plunder the island's treasures for personal gain, while Professor von Braun aims to harness its knowledge for his own scientific ambitions. Lady Seraphina, meanwhile, seeks to exploit the island's mystical powers for her dark purposes.

Amidst the crew's own ranks, they uncover instances of betrayal and deception. A trusted crew member is revealed to be secretly colluding with the rival adventurers, exchanging information for promises of riches and power. Another crew member harbors personal ambitions that threaten to jeopardize the safety and success of the mission.

In their interactions with indigenous peoples, Captain Amelia and her crew uncover hidden agendas driven by centuries-old conflicts and rivalries. They navigate delicate negotiations and uncover long-standing grievances that must be addressed in order to secure alliances and access vital resources.

As hidden agendas come to light, Captain Amelia and her crew are faced with ethical dilemmas that challenge their principles and convictions. They must grapple with difficult decisions about how to proceed, weighing the potential consequences of their actions and striving to uphold their values in the face of temptation and adversity.

Despite the revelations of hidden agendas and betrayals, Captain Amelia and her crew remain steadfast in their commitment to their quest for knowledge. They confront these challenges with courage and resolve, determined to overcome obstacles and continue their journey towards the Island of Knowledge, guided by the belief that truth and integrity will ultimately prevail.

As The Voyager sails onward, Captain Amelia and her crew confront the steep price of ambition, witnessing firsthand the consequences of unchecked desire and ruthless ambition.

In the pursuit of power and knowledge, rival adventurers and treasure hunters abandon their morals and principles, resorting to deceit, betrayal, and exploitation. Their relentless pursuit of personal gain leads them down a dark path, blinding them to the ethical implications of their actions and leaving devastation in their wake.

Ambition drives wedges between allies and fractures once-strong relationships. Betrayals and hidden agendas sow seeds of mistrust among Captain Amelia's crew, threatening to tear apart the bonds of friendship and camaraderie that have sustained them thus far. As loyalties are tested and allegiances shift, the crew must confront the painful reality of betrayal from within their own ranks.

The relentless pursuit of ambition consumes the hearts and minds of those who succumb to its allure, leading them to sacrifice their humanity in exchange for power and prestige. As rival adventurers descend deeper into darkness, they lose touch with their empathy and compassion, becoming ruthless and merciless in their quest to achieve their goals.

The price of ambition extends beyond the immediate pursuit of power and knowledge, unleashing unforeseen consequences that ripple outward and impact all who are touched by its influence. The actions of the ambitious have far-reaching ramifications, causing harm to innocent bystanders and destabilizing the delicate balance of the world around them.

As Captain Amelia and her crew bear witness to the price of ambition, they are reminded of the importance of staying true to their values and principles, even in the face of overwhelming temptation. They understand that while ambition may promise riches and glory, the true measure of greatness lies not in the treasures amassed, but in the integrity and honor with which one conducts oneself along the way.

Throughout their journey aboard The Voyager, Captain Amelia and her crew have gleaned invaluable lessons in integrity and honor, shaping their understanding of themselves and the world around them.

In the end, the lessons in integrity and honor learned aboard The Voyager have not only guided Captain Amelia and her crew on their quest for knowledge but have also transformed them into individuals of character and integrity, ready to face whatever challenges the future may hold with dignity and grace.

EPISODE FIVE

Ep 5

As The Voyager sails into the final leg of its epic journey, Captain Amelia and her crew brace themselves for the challenges and revelations that lie ahead. With the Island of Knowledge tantalizingly close on the horizon, tensions run high as the crew prepares for the culmination of their quest. But amidst the anticipation, there is also a sense of trepidation as they confront the unknown dangers that await them. Rival adventurers and treacherous waters threaten to derail their mission at any moment, testing their resolve and pushing them to their limits.

Yet, as The Voyager presses onward, Captain Amelia remains steadfast in her determination to reach the island and unlock its secrets. For she knows that the answers they seek answers to the universe's greatest mysteries lie just beyond the horizon, waiting to be discovered.

And so, with courage in their hearts and the wind at their backs, Captain Amelia and her crew set sail into the final leg of their journey, ready to face whatever challenges come their way in their relentless pursuit of knowledge and truth.

As The Voyager approaches the fabled Island of Knowledge, a sense of awe and anticipation fills the hearts of Captain Amelia and her crew. After countless trials and tribulations, they have finally reached their destination, standing on the threshold of unlocking the universe's greatest mysteries.

As the island's shores come into view, they are greeted by a landscape shrouded in mystery and wonder. Towering cliffs rise from the sea, adorned with ancient ruins and hidden chambers waiting to be explored. The air is thick with the scent of adventure, and the promise of discovery hangs palpably in the air.

But amidst the excitement, there is also a sense of reverence as Captain Amelia and her crew step foot on the hallowed ground of the Island of Knowledge. They approach its shores with humility and respect, mindful of the sacred knowledge that lies hidden within its depths.

With each step forward, they embark on a journey of exploration and enlightenment, uncovering the secrets of the island's ancient past and unlocking the mysteries of the universe. From ancient texts and inscriptions to forgotten artifacts and relics, they delve deep into the heart of the island, guided by their insatiable thirst for knowledge.

And as they journey deeper into the island's interior, Captain Amelia and her crew come to realize that the true treasures of the Island of Knowledge are not found in gold or jewels, but in the wisdom and understanding they gain along the way. For in the end, it is not just the destination that matters, but the journey itself a journey filled with discovery, wonder, and the boundless pursuit of knowledge.

As Captain Amelia and her crew set foot on the fabled Island of Knowledge, they are immediately drawn to the ancient ruins that dot its landscape, each one holding the promise of untold secrets and hidden knowledge.

With eager anticipation, they begin their exploration, venturing deep into the heart of the ruins with a sense of reverence and awe. The crumbling walls and weathered stone speak of civilizations long forgotten, their mysteries waiting to be uncovered by intrepid explorers.

As they traverse the ancient corridors and crumbling passageways, Captain Amelia and her crew discover a wealth of artifacts and relics, each one a testament to the island's rich history and storied past. From intricately carved statues to ancient manuscripts and scrolls, they piece together fragments of a lost civilization, slowly unraveling the mysteries of its rise and fall.

But amidst the treasures they uncover, they also encounter challenges and obstacles that test their resolve and ingenuity. Collapsing tunnels, hidden traps, and ancient guardians stand between them and the knowledge they seek, forcing them to rely on their wits and resourcefulness to overcome each new obstacle.

Yet, with each step forward, Captain Amelia and her crew come closer to unlocking the secrets of the island and uncovering the truths that lie hidden within its ancient ruins. And as they delve deeper into the mysteries of the past, they come to realize that the greatest discoveries are not found in gold or jewels, but in the wisdom and understanding they gain along the way.

As Captain Amelia and her crew explore the ancient ruins on the Island of Knowledge, they uncover hidden chambers that hold the promise of even greater mysteries and revelations.

Venturing deeper into the heart of the ruins, they stumble upon concealed passageways and secret entrances, concealed from the prying eyes of the outside world for centuries. With each discovery, their excitement mounts, knowing that they are drawing closer to uncovering the island's most closely guarded secrets.

As they enter these hidden chambers, they are greeted by sights that defy imagination. Ornate carvings adorn the walls, depicting scenes of ancient rituals and ceremonies long forgotten. Strange symbols and inscriptions cover every surface, hinting at the knowledge and wisdom that lies hidden within.

But the true treasures of these hidden chambers are not material riches, but the knowledge and understanding they contain. Captain Amelia and her crew pore over ancient texts and scrolls, deciphering cryptic passages and piecing together fragments of a lost civilization's history.

Yet, with each new revelation comes new questions and new challenges. Ancient puzzles and riddles test their intellect and wit, requiring them to think creatively and work together to unlock the secrets that lie hidden within.

And as they delve deeper into the mysteries of the hidden chambers, Captain Amelia and her crew come to realize that the true value of their journey lies not just in the treasures they uncover, but in the wisdom and understanding they gain along the way. For in the end, it is the pursuit of knowledge that is the greatest treasure of all.

As Captain Amelia and her crew uncover the long-hidden secrets of the Island of Knowledge, they are astounded by the depth and breadth of the revelations they encounter.

Delving into ancient texts and inscriptions, they uncover the island's role as a repository of knowledge about the origins of existence. They learn of ancient myths and cosmologies that offer insights into the creation of the universe and the forces that govern it.

Within the hidden chambers of the island, they discover the source of its mystical power, a rare and potent energy that has fueled the island's secrets for millennia. They come to understand how this energy has shaped the island's history and influenced the development of civilizations throughout time.

Through encounters with enigmatic guardians who protect the island's secrets, Captain Amelia and her crew learn of the ancient order tasked with safeguarding the island's knowledge. They uncover the guardians' role as stewards of wisdom, entrusted with preserving the island's secrets for future generations.

Exploring the island's vast archives and libraries, they gain access to a wealth of knowledge spanning a multitude of disciplines. They discover that the island's secrets encompass not only scientific and scholarly pursuits but also spiritual and philosophical insights, revealing a holistic understanding of the world and humanity's place within it.

As they delve deeper into the island's mysteries, Captain Amelia and her crew confront ethical dilemmas that challenge their principles and values. They grapple with the responsibility that comes with possessing such profound knowledge, wrestling with questions of how to use it for the betterment of humanity while avoiding its exploitation for selfish gain.

In the end, the secrets of the Island of Knowledge reveal themselves to be both awe-inspiring and humbling, offering Captain Amelia and her crew a profound glimpse into the mysteries of the universe and the complexities of the human experience. Armed with this newfound understanding, they set sail once more, emboldened by the wisdom they have gained and the adventures that still await them on the horizon.

As Captain Amelia and her crew ventured deeper into the heart of the Island of Knowledge, a sense of anticipation tingled in the air. The ancient ruins loomed before them, their weathered stone walls whispering secrets of civilizations long past. Amidst the crumbling structures, they uncovered artifacts that hinted at the island's profound mysteries. Intricately carved tablets depicted celestial maps charting the movements of stars and galaxies. Fragments of ancient texts spoke of philosophical teachings that promised to illuminate the nature of existence itself.

As they delved deeper into the island's hidden chambers, they encountered relics of advanced technology that surpassed anything they had ever seen. Mysterious devices hummed with energy, their purpose shrouded in mystery. Captain Amelia and her crew marveled at the ingenuity of the ancient builders, realizing that they stood on the threshold of discoveries that could reshape the world.

But amidst the excitement of their discoveries, there was also a sense of reverence. They understood that with knowledge came responsibility, the responsibility to use their newfound wisdom for the betterment of humanity, and to guard against the dangers of hubris and greed.

And so, with hearts full of hope and minds hungry for understanding, Captain Amelia and her crew pressed onward, knowing that the greatest discoveries of their journey still lay ahead, waiting to be uncovered in the depths of the Island of Knowledge.

As the Voyager ventured further into uncharted waters, the air was thick with anticipation and uncertainty. Captain Amelia stood at the helm, her gaze fixed on the horizon ahead. Around her, the crew moved with purpose, their expressions a mixture of excitement and apprehension.

The sea stretched out before them, vast and unfathomable, its depths hiding secrets known only to the bravest of explorers. With each passing moment, they sailed further from the safety of familiar shores, confronting the unknown with a sense of both awe and trepidation.

As night fell, the sky darkened, and the stars emerged, casting their ethereal glow upon the water. Yet, even as the crew marveled at the celestial display above, a sense of unease lingered in the air. They knew that beyond the reach of their lanterns lay a realm of darkness and mystery, where anything could lurk beneath the waves.

Suddenly, a fierce gust of wind whipped through the sails, sending The Voyager lurching violently to one side. The crew sprang into action, their training and instinct guiding them as they battled to keep the ship steady amidst the chaos of the storm.

Amidst the howling winds and crashing waves, Captain Amelia and her crew confronted the unknown with courage and determination, knowing that they were bound together by a common purpose: the relentless pursuit of knowledge and discovery, no matter the cost.

And so, as The Voyager sailed ever deeper into the uncharted waters, Captain Amelia and her crew braced themselves for whatever challenges the unknown might throw their way, ready to face them with unwavering resolve and indomitable spirit.

In the twilight hours of the day, as the sun dipped below the horizon, The Voyager sailed onward into the vast expanse of the open sea. Captain Amelia stood at the helm, her eyes fixed on the distant horizon, her mind abuzz with anticipation for what lay ahead.

As the ship cut through the waves, the crew bustled about, preparing for the night's journey into the unknown. There was an air of excitement aboard The Voyager, for they knew that they were on the brink of something extraordinary.

As night fell and the stars emerged from their hiding places, casting their shimmering light upon the water, Captain Amelia called her crew together on the deck. With a solemn yet determined voice, she spoke of their mission to seek out the depths of wisdom that lay hidden beneath the surface of the ocean.

With each passing moment, The Voyager sailed deeper into the heart of the ocean, leaving behind the familiar shores of civilization and venturing into uncharted waters. The crew marveled at the vastness of the sea, its depths shrouded in mystery and wonder.

As they sailed onward, Captain Amelia and her crew encountered strange and wondrous sights beneath the waves, ancient ruins covered in coral, schools of brightly colored fish darting through the water, and vast underwater caverns teeming with life.

But amidst the beauty of the ocean, there was also danger lurking in the depths. The crew encountered fierce storms and treacherous currents that threatened to pull them under, testing their courage and resolve.

Yet, through it all, Captain Amelia and her crew pressed onward, driven by their insatiable thirst for knowledge and understanding. For they knew that the depths of wisdom held the answers to life's greatest questions, and they were determined to uncover them, no matter the cost.

And so, as The Voyager sailed deeper into the unknown, Captain Amelia and her crew embraced the challenges that lay ahead, knowing that their journey would lead them to the very heart of enlightenment and truth.

As the Voyager continued its voyage into uncharted waters, Captain Amelia and her crew encountered a new challenge: the complexities of interpretation.

Amidst the ancient ruins they explored, Captain Amelia and her crew discovered texts and symbols etched into stone tablets and carvings. These inscriptions held the promise of great knowledge, but their meanings were often obscured by the passage of time and the enigmatic nature of ancient languages.

As they delved deeper into their studies, Captain Amelia and her crew realized that their own cultural biases and assumptions could cloud their interpretation of the ancient texts. They had to learn to approach the texts with an open mind, willing to consider alternate perspectives and interpretations.

Many of the symbols and motifs they encountered had symbolic meanings that were deeply rooted in the beliefs and traditions of the ancient civilizations that created them. Captain Amelia and her crew had to decipher the symbolic language of the ancients, unraveling the hidden meanings behind each intricate design.

In order to fully grasp the significance of the ancient texts and symbols, Captain Amelia and her crew had to consider the historical and cultural context in which they were created. They studied the archaeological evidence surrounding the ruins, piecing together clues that shed light on the beliefs and practices of the ancient civilizations.

As they delved deeper into their studies, Captain Amelia and her crew grappled with ethical considerations surrounding the interpretation of the ancient texts. They questioned their own biases and motivations, striving to approach their work with integrity and respect for the cultures that had come before them.

Despite the challenges they faced, Captain Amelia and her crew persevered in their quest for knowledge, knowing that the secrets of the ancient world held the key to unlocking the mysteries of the universe. And as they continued their journey, they gained a deeper understanding of the complexities of interpretation and the importance of approaching their work with humility and reverence.

As The Voyager's journey into the unknown drew to a close, Captain Amelia and her crew gathered on the deck to reflect on the challenges, triumphs, and revelations they had experienced along the way.

Amidst the trials and tribulations they faced, Captain Amelia and her crew forged bonds of friendship and camaraderie that would last a lifetime. They had stood together in the face of danger, supported each other through moments of uncertainty, and celebrated their victories as one united crew. Each member of the crew reflected on the lessons they had learned throughout their journey, the importance of perseverance in the face of adversity, the value of teamwork and cooperation, and the humility to acknowledge the vastness of the unknown.

As they looked back on their journey, Captain Amelia and her crew realized that they had undergone profound personal transformations. They had been tested in ways they never thought possible, and had emerged stronger, wiser, and more resilient than ever before.

Despite the challenges they had faced, Captain Amelia and her crew expressed gratitude for the experience of a lifetime. They knew that their journey had been a privileged one that few ever had the opportunity to undertake and they cherished every moment they had spent together aboard The Voyager.

As they prepared to return to civilization, Captain Amelia and her crew looked to the future with a sense of hope and optimism. They knew that their journey had only just begun, that there were still countless mysteries waiting to be uncovered, and adventures waiting to be had.

And so, as The Voyager sailed homeward, Captain Amelia and her crew carried with them the memories of their journey into the unknown, the challenges they had overcome, the friendships they had forged, and the wisdom they had gained along the way. And though their voyage had come to an end, they knew that the spirit of exploration and discovery would live on in their hearts forever.

As the Voyager departed from the Island of Knowledge, Captain Amelia and her crew reflected on the profound legacy left behind by their journey.

Through their exploration of the island's ancient ruins and hidden chambers, Captain Amelia and her crew had unearthed a treasure trove of knowledge that would forever change the course of history. They knew that the wisdom they had gained would be passed down through the ages, inspiring future generations of scholars, scientists, and adventurers.

The crew recognized that their interactions with the island's guardians and the indigenous inhabitants had fostered a spirit of cultural exchange and understanding. They had learned from each other, sharing stories, traditions, and knowledge that transcended language and cultural barriers.

Captain Amelia and her crew were deeply moved by the island's commitment to environmental harmony and sustainability. They vowed to carry forward the lessons they had learned about the importance of preserving and protecting the natural world, ensuring that future generations would inherit a planet rich in biodiversity and beauty.

The crew grappled with the ethical dilemmas posed by their quest for knowledge and power. They understood the importance of using their newfound wisdom for the betterment of humanity, and they pledged to uphold the principles of integrity, compassion, and humility in all their future endeavors.

Above all, Captain Amelia and her crew recognized the legacy of exploration and discovery that their journey had inspired. They knew that their voyage into the unknown had paved the way for future adventurers to follow in their footsteps, venturing into uncharted waters in search of truth, wisdom, and enlightenment.

As The Voyager sailed into the sunset, Captain Amelia and her crew carried with them the legacy of the Island of Knowledge, a legacy of knowledge, understanding, and enlightenment that would endure for generations to come. And though their journey had come to an end, they knew that the spirit of exploration and discovery would live on in the hearts and minds of all who dared to seek the unknown.

EPISODE SIX

Ep 6

As The Voyager sailed steadily toward the horizon, Captain Amelia stood at the bow, her gaze fixed on the distant shores that marked the end of their long journey. Behind her, the crew bustled about the deck, their faces drawn with a mixture of anticipation and sadness.

For months, they had sailed the open seas, braving storms and facing unknown dangers in pursuit of knowledge and enlightenment. Now, as they approached their final destination, a sense of finality hung in the air, mingled with a bittersweet longing for the adventures that lay behind them.

As the sun dipped low in the sky, casting its golden rays upon the water, Captain Amelia felt a surge of emotion welling up within her. She thought of all they had accomplished together the challenges they had overcome, the discoveries they had made, and the bonds of friendship they had forged along the way.

And as The Voyager drew ever closer to the shores of their journey's end, Captain Amelia knew that their adventure was far from over. For though their voyage may be coming to a close, the memories they had made and the lessons they had learned would stay with them always, guiding them

on new adventures yet to come.

As The Voyager approached the shores of the Island of Secrets, anticipation coursed through the crew like electricity. They had embarked on this journey fueled by curiosity, driven by the promise of unlocking mysteries that had eluded scholars and adventurers for generations.

As the island's silhouette emerged on the horizon, Captain Amelia gathered her crew on deck. With a voice filled with determination, she reminded them of the importance of their quest to uncover the island's long-hidden secrets and unlock the knowledge that lay buried within its ancient ruins.

As The Voyager anchored offshore, Captain Amelia and her crew prepared to set foot on the island's shores. With each step they took, they felt a palpable sense of excitement and wonder, knowing that they were about to embark on the adventure of a lifetime.

Exploring the island's dense jungle and rugged terrain, they encountered clues and artifacts that hinted at the island's enigmatic past. They discovered crumbling temples and weathered statues, each one holding a piece of the puzzle they were determined to solve.

As they delved deeper into the island's secrets, Captain Amelia and her crew encountered challenges and obstacles that tested their resolve and ingenuity. They faced ancient traps and puzzles designed to guard the island's treasures, but they pressed on undeterred, driven by their thirst for knowledge and understanding.

And then, at last, they made their greatest discovery: a hidden chamber deep within the heart of the island, filled with scrolls and manuscripts containing the wisdom of ages past. With trembling hands, they unrolled the ancient texts, eager to unlock the secrets they held within.

As they pored over the ancient writings, Captain Amelia and her crew realized that the true treasure of the island was not gold or jewels, but the knowledge and wisdom they had uncovered. For in the end, it was not the material riches that mattered, but the journey of discovery and enlightenment they

had undertaken together.

As Captain Amelia and her crew delved

deeper into the mysteries of the Island of

Secrets, they underwent profound personal

transformations, each member experiencing

a journey of self-discovery and growth.

Throughout the voyage, Captain Amelia's

leadership was tested like never before. She

faced challenges with unwavering resolve, guiding her crew with wisdom and determination. Through the trials and tribulations they encountered, she emerged as a stronger and more confident leader, ready to face whatever challenges lay ahead. Among the crew were scholars and academics hungry for knowledge. As they uncovered the island's secrets, they found not only answers to their questions but also a deeper understanding of themselves and their place in the world. Their pursuit of knowledge became more than just an academic endeavor; it became a journey of personal enlightenment and self-discovery.

For the adventurers among them, the journey was a test of courage and resilience. They faced dangers both physical and emotional, confronting their fears and pushing themselves to their limits. Through their trials, they discovered a newfound strength within themselves, proving that they were capable of overcoming even the most daunting challenges.

The scientists aboard The Voyager approached the journey with an insatiable curiosity and a thirst for discovery. As they unraveled the island's mysteries, they found themselves questioning their assumptions and expanding their understanding of the natural world. Their scientific curiosity led them to new realms of knowledge and understanding, forever changing the way they saw the world around them.

Throughout the journey, each member of the crew was humbled by the vastness of the unknown and the mysteries that lay beyond their comprehension. They realized that true wisdom came not from arrogance or pride, but from humility and an openness to learning from the world around them. In the end, they emerged from their journey transformed not only by the knowledge they had gained but by the journey of self-discovery they had undertaken together.

As The Voyager neared the fabled Island of Secrets, Captain Amelia and her crew found themselves grappling with profound ethical implications that shadowed their journey like a looming storm.

As whispers of the island's legendary secrets spread among the crew, a palpable excitement tinged with apprehension rippled through The Voyager. Yet, with the promise of unlocking mysteries that had eluded humanity for centuries came the temptation to prioritize personal enlightenment over the greater good.

Upon setting foot on the island's pristine shores, the crew was struck by its untouched beauty and delicate ecosystem. They faced a moral dilemma: how could they balance their quest for knowledge with the responsibility to protect and preserve the island's natural wonders for future generations?

Encountering the island's indigenous inhabitants, Captain Amelia and her crew were reminded of the importance of respecting their culture, traditions, and sovereignty. They grappled with the ethical imperative to engage with the indigenous community on equal terms, acknowledging their rights to self-determination and land stewardship.

As they delved deeper into the island's mysteries, the crew confronted the ethical imperative of transparency and accountability. They questioned the implications of their discoveries and wrestled with the moral obligation to share their findings openly and honestly with the world, rather than hoarding them for personal gain.

With each revelation uncovered on the island, Captain Amelia and her crew were forced to confront the moral cost of their pursuit of knowledge. They questioned whether the pursuit of enlightenment justified the potential consequences, both for themselves and for the world at large.

Amidst the swirling currents of ethical uncertainty, Captain Amelia and her crew found themselves navigating uncharted waters not only in search of knowledge but also in search of moral clarity and integrity. For in the crucible of their journey, they discovered that the true measure of their worth lay not only in what they uncovered but in how they chose to confront the ethical implications of their discoveries.

As the Voyager pressed onward toward the Island of Secrets, Captain Amelia and her crew found themselves immersed in a journey that transcended the mere pursuit of knowledge. It became a quest to confront the very essence of human understanding and grapple with the mysteries that lay beyond.

With each step they took on the island's ancient soil, the crew felt a profound sense of humility wash over them. They gazed upon the towering ruins and intricate carvings, realizing that they stood on the precipice of knowledge so vast and profound that it defied comprehension.

As they delved deeper into the island's secrets, Captain Amelia and her crew encountered phenomena that stretched the limits of their understanding. They witnessed strange anomalies and inexplicable occurrences that challenged their perception of reality, forcing them to confront the inherent limitations of human cognition.

Amidst the ancient ruins, Captain Amelia and her crew engaged in deep philosophical discussions, contemplating the nature of existence and the mysteries of the cosmos. They grappled with questions that had plagued humanity for eons, pondering the nature of consciousness, the meaning of life, and the possibility of otherworldly realms beyond their comprehension.

Yet, amidst the uncertainty and doubt, Captain Amelia and her crew found solace in the beauty of the unknown. They embraced the notion that some truths were meant to remain elusive, and that the journey of discovery was as much about the questions as it was about the answers.

As The Voyager journeyed toward the Island of Secrets, Captain Amelia and her crew experienced a series of epiphanies that reshaped their understanding of the world and their place within it.

Amidst the vast expanse of the ocean, the crew marveled at the interconnectedness of all living beings. They realized that every action, no matter how small, had ripple effects that reverberated throughout the world, connecting them to the web of life that spanned the globe.

Facing challenges together, Captain Amelia and her crew discovered the strength that came from unity and solidarity. They realized that by working together, they could overcome obstacles that seemed insurmountable, forging bonds of friendship and camaraderie that would endure long after their journey had ended.

Encountering the diverse cultures and ecosystems of the world, the crew came to appreciate the beauty and richness of diversity. They understood that it was our differences that made us unique, and that by embracing diversity, they could learn and grow in ways they had never imagined.

Confronting the raw power of nature, Captain Amelia and her crew witnessed the fragility of human existence in the face of forces beyond their control. They realized that life was precious and fleeting, and that every moment should be cherished and savored to the fullest.

Despite facing adversity and hardship, Captain Amelia and her crew were inspired by the resilience of the human spirit. They witnessed acts of courage, kindness, and compassion that reaffirmed their faith in humanity and gave them hope for the future. In the end, as The Voyager sailed ever closer to its destination, Captain Amelia and her crew carried with them the lessons they had learned and the epiphanies they had experienced along the way. They knew that their journey was not just about reaching the Island of Secrets, but about the transformative power of exploration, discovery, and self-discovery along the way.

As The Voyager charted its course through uncharted waters, Captain Amelia and her crew embraced humility as a guiding principle on their journey of discovery.

In the face of vast expanses of ocean and unexplored territories, Captain Amelia and her crew humbly acknowledged the limits of their knowledge. They understood that the mysteries of the world were vast and that their understanding was but a drop in the ocean of human understanding. Amidst the awe inspiring beauty of the natural world, Captain Amelia and her crew found solace in the humility of nature. They marveled at the grandeur of towering mountains, the vastness of endless horizons, and the intricate complexity of ecosystems. In these moments, they recognized their own smallness in the face of nature's majesty.

Encountering diverse cultures and peoples along their journey, Captain Amelia and her crew approached each interaction with humility and an open mind. They recognized the richness of human experience and the value of learning from those whose perspectives differed from their own.

When encountering indigenous communities, Captain Amelia and her crew approached with reverence and respect for their ancestral knowledge and traditions. They understood that these communities held deep wisdom passed down through generations and sought to learn from their insights into the natural world.

Throughout their voyage, Captain Amelia and her crew experienced setbacks and failures. Instead of viewing these as obstacles, they embraced them as opportunities for growth and learning. Through humility, they recognized their own fallibility and committed to approaching challenges with resilience and grace.

In the end, as The Voyager sailed onward, Captain Amelia and her crew found strength in their humility. They understood that true wisdom came not from arrogance or certainty, but from a willingness to embrace the unknown with open hearts and minds. And as they journeyed onward, they did so with a sense of humility that would guide them through the ever-unfolding mysteries of their voyage.

As The Voyager continued its voyage, Captain Amelia and her crew gradually uncovered the essence of true wisdom amidst the challenges and revelations of their journey.

True wisdom, they realized, was not merely about possessing knowledge, but about nurturing a lifelong curiosity and thirst for learning. Each new discovery on their journey fueled their curiosity and propelled them forward in their quest for understanding.

Along their journey, Captain Amelia and her crew learned the importance of empathy, the ability to understand and share the feelings of others. They realized that true wisdom required not only intellectual understanding but also emotional intelligence and compassion for fellow beings.

Humility, they discovered, was a cornerstone of true wisdom. It was the recognition of one's own limitations and the willingness to learn from others, to admit mistakes, and to approach the world with openness and humility.

As they navigated the vastness of the ocean and the mysteries of the Island of Secrets, Captain Amelia and her crew sought deeper meaning and purpose in their journey. They realized that true wisdom lay in understanding one's place in the universe and living a life aligned with one's values and principles.

Ultimately, Captain Amelia and her crew came to understand that true wisdom was not an individual pursuit but a collective endeavor. It was about fostering connections with nature, with others, and with the greater cosmos that transcended boundaries and enriched their lives in profound ways.

In the end, as The Voyager sailed ever onward, Captain Amelia and her crew carried with them the realization that true wisdom was not a destination to be reached but a journey to be embraced, a journey of curiosity, empathy, humility, meaning, and connection that would continue to unfold with each passing day. And with this understanding, they navigated the seas of uncertainty with a newfound sense of purpose and clarity, ready to face whatever challenges lay ahead on their quest for true wisdom.

As The Voyager's journey neared its conclusion, Captain Amelia and her crew took a moment to reflect on the profound experiences and lessons learned along their quest.

Amidst the challenges and triumphs, Captain Amelia and her crew felt a deep sense of gratitude for the opportunity to embark on such an extraordinary adventure. They cherished the memories of camaraderie, discovery, and growth that had shaped their journey.

Reflecting on the vastness of the ocean and the mysteries of the Island of Secrets, the crew embraced humility in the face of the unknown. They acknowledged that their quest had only scratched the surface of the boundless depths of the universe, and that there would always be more to explore and discover.

Throughout their journey, Captain Amelia and her crew had faced countless challenges and obstacles. Yet, they had persevered with courage and resilience, overcoming adversity through teamwork, determination, and unwavering resolve.

As they traveled the seas and explored distant shores, the crew felt a deepening connection to the natural world and to their fellow human beings. They realized that, despite their differences, they were all united by a shared sense of wonder, curiosity, and longing for understanding.

As they prepared to return to civilization, Captain Amelia and her crew felt a renewed sense of purpose and vision. They understood that their quest for knowledge and wisdom was not confined to the confines of the ship or the shores of the island, but extended far beyond, into the vast expanse of the universe itself.

In the end, as The Voyager sailed homeward, Captain Amelia and her crew carried with them the memories of their journey, the lessons of their quest, and a deep-seated conviction that the pursuit of knowledge and understanding was a journey worth undertaking, no matter the challenges or uncertainties that lay ahead. And with this understanding, they embarked on the next chapter of their lives, ready to face whatever adventures awaited them with courage, curiosity, and an unyielding spirit of exploration.

As The Voyager sailed into uncharted waters, Captain Amelia and her crew embraced the unknown with a mixture of trepidation and excitement, knowing that their journey would be fraught with uncertainty yet filled with endless possibilities.

Despite the daunting prospect of venturing into unknown territories, Captain Amelia and her crew found the courage to confront their fears head-on. They understood that true growth and discovery often required stepping out of their comfort zones and embracing the unknown with open hearts and minds.

As they sailed farther from familiar shores, the crew embraced the spirit of adventure that stirred within their souls. They relished the opportunity to explore new horizons, encounter new cultures, and discover hidden treasures that lay beyond the reaches of their imagination.

Along their journey, Captain Amelia and her crew encountered unforeseen challenges and obstacles that tested their resilience and resolve. Yet, with each setback, they learned to adapt, persevere, and emerge stronger than before, knowing that every trial was an opportunity for growth and learning.

Amidst the vast expanse of the unknown, the crew discovered beauty in the most unexpected places. They marveled at the awe-inspiring sights of unexplored landscapes, the breathtaking wonders of untouched nature, and the profound mysteries that lurked beneath the surface of the unfamiliar.

Ultimately, Captain Amelia and her crew learned to embrace the journey itself, with all its twists and turns, uncertainties and surprises. They understood that life was an adventure to be lived to the fullest, and that the unknown held endless opportunities for discovery, growth, and transformation.

As The Voyager sailed onward into the unknown, Captain Amelia and her crew faced the future with courage, curiosity, and a sense of wonder, knowing that whatever challenges awaited them, they would navigate them together, united in their shared quest for adventure, discovery, and the pursuit of the unknown.

www.ingramcontent.com/pod-product-compliance
Lightning Source LLC
Chambersburg PA
CBHW061626250726
48659CB00004B/1099